thinking of You

COLORING BOOK

artwork
by
joy hall

HARVEST HOUSE PUBLISHERS
EUGENE, OREGON

Cover by Connie Gabbert Design + Illustration

THINKING OF YOU COLORING BOOK

Artwork copyright © 2016 by Joy Hall
Published by Harvest House Publishers
Eugene, Oregon 97402
www.harvesthousepublishers.com

ISBN 978-0-7369-6951-2 (pbk.)

Printed in United States of America

16 17 18 19 20 21 22 23 / UG-JC / 10 9 8 7 6 5 4 3 2 1

Deliver Color and Joy to Someone Special

Express yourself and your heart for others by adding your colorful touch to these beautifully illustrated cards and prints. Personalize each original design using markers, watercolors, crayons, or colored pencils. Simply detach and color a beautiful illustration and send it into the world.

Having this one-stop collection of cards and prints means that you'll always know where to go for personal birthday, thank you, friendship, sympathy, love, congratulations, and special holiday gifts. Send a friend a birthday card featuring a bouquet of her favorite shades. Congratulate a bride and groom with a framed inspiration in their wedding colors. Let each of your kids paint a different Christmas image for Grandpa to give him plenty of cheer to decorate the mantel.

The simple DIYs for envelopes and frames give you even more personalized options. Color it and mail it. Color it and frame it. (You can even color it and keep it!) Or deliver an uncolored design along with a set of markers to surprise someone with an afternoon of creative fun.

Have a great time. You don't have to be an artist to create and share art from the heart!

About the Artist

Joy Hall is a professional artist for the gift and home decor markets. Her exquisite watercolors can be seen on a wide variety of products including dinnerware, calendars, garden flags, kitchen textiles, quilting fabric, and greeting cards. She's a Texas city girl living in the Pennsylvania countryside with her wonderful husband and two sons. Visit the artist at www.joyhallart.com.

We'd love to see your creations!
Share your finished projects on social media with the hashtag

#DIYgifts

We'll be looking for your artwork!

For information on more Harvest House
coloring books for adults, please visit

www.harvesthousepublishers.com

HAPPY BIRTHDAY

HOORAY   YIPEE

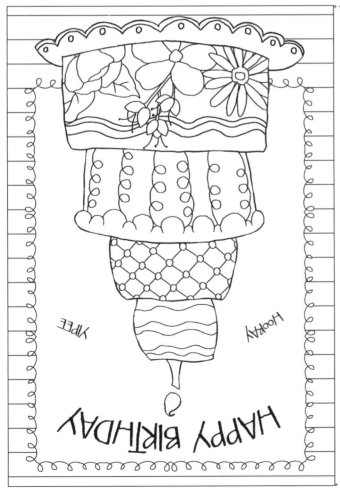

HAPPY BIRTHDAY

YIPEE   HOORAY

We turn not older
WITH YEARS
but newer
EVERY DAY.

EMILY DICKINSON

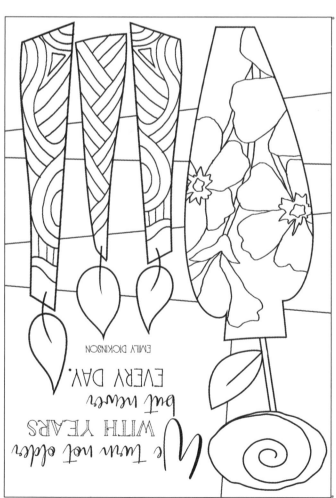

Happy Birthday, FRIEND.

FRIENDS ARE THE SUNSHINE OF LIFE.

JOHN HAY

LOVE IS FLOWER-LIKE; Friendship is A SHELTERING TREE.

SAMUEL TAYLOR COLERIDGE

Many kinds OF FRUIT GROW UPON the tree of life. BUT NONE SO SWEET AS friendship.

LUCY LARCOM

OF ALL *the best things* UPON EARTH, I HOLD *that a faithful friend* IS THE *best*.

OWEN MEREDITH

OF ALL *the best things* UPON EARTH, I HOLD *that a faithful friend* IS THE *best*.

OWEN MEREDITH

If instead of a gem, or even a flower, we should cast the gift of a loving thought into the heart of a friend, that would be giving as the angels give.

GEORGE MACDONALD

Let us be
GRATEFUL
To people
WHO MAKE US
HAPPY;
they are the
CHARMING GARDENERS
WHO MAKE
OUR SOULS
blossom.

MARCEL PROUST

Let us be
GRATEFUL
To people
WHO MAKE US
HAPPY;
they are the
CHARMING GARDENERS
WHO MAKE
OUR SOULS
blossom.

MARCEL PROUST

Thank you
FOR YOUR
KINDNESS.

Thank you
FOR YOUR
KINDNESS.

MAY your heart BE HELD BY COMFORT & care

WITH DEEPEST SYMPATHY.

Your promise REVIVES ME; IT COMFORTS ME IN ALL MY TROUBLES.

PSALM 119:50

CONGRATULATIONS

YOU DID IT!

OUR ASPIRATIONS ARE OUR POSSIBILITIES.

SAMUEL JOHNSON

CONGRATULATIONS

YOU DID IT!

OUR ASPIRATIONS ARE OUR POSSIBILITIES.

SAMUEL JOHNSON

To love.
AND TO BE LOVED,
is the greatest happiness
OF EXISTENCE.
♡
SYDNEY SMITH

To love.
AND TO BE LOVED,
is the greatest happiness
OF EXISTENCE.
♡
SYDNEY SMITH

Love
BEARS ALL THINGS,
believes ALL THINGS,
HOPES
ALL THINGS,
ENDURES all things
LOVE
NEVER FAILS.

1 CORINTHIANS 13:7-8

Hallelujah,
HE IS RISEN!
LET US REJOICE
with song
AND
GRATITUDE.

Hallelujah,
HE IS RISEN!
LET US REJOICE
with song
AND
GRATITUDE.

I REMEMBER
MY MOTHER'S
prayers
AND THEY HAVE ALWAYS
FOLLOWED ME.
They have
CLUNG TO ME
ALL MY LIFE.
ABRAHAM LINCOLN

A mother's arms
ARE MADE OF
TENDERNESS.
VICTOR HUGO

HUNDREDS OF DEWDROPS TO GREET THE DAWN,
HUNDREDS OF BEES IN THE PURPLE CLOVER,
HUNDREDS OF BUTTERFLIES
ON THE LAWN,

BUT ONLY
ONE
Mother
THE WIDE WORLD OVER.

GEORGE COOPER

May you experience THE PEACE AND WONDER of this HOLY SEASON.

May you experience THE PEACE AND WONDER of this HOLY SEASON.

For to us a child is born...

AND HE WILL BE CALLED
Wonderful COUNSELOR,
MIGHTY GOD,
Everlasting Father.
PRINCE OF PEACE.
ISAIAH 9:6

O HOLY NIGHT,
The stars
ARE BRIGHTLY
SHINING;
IT IS THE NIGHT
of the dear
SAVIOR'S
birth.